Praise for *call mother a lonely field*

'A tale from a dark and troubled place—Belfast in the book comes from love and language. Liam Carson's intense portrayal of his parents and the divided city enriched no matter your origins.'

—Bernard MacLaverty

'Raymond Carver used to say one good short story was worth any number of bad novels. So with Liam Carson's short pearl of a book — worth any number of heavy tomes... The book scoops up hot embers and implosive elements of a time when language became a kind of lightning rod and secret preserve for the spirit.'

—Tess Gallagher

'Like the city he grew up in, Liam Carson's memoir of life in Belfast winds like a tangled web of streets, dreams, cultures and philosophies, where every page, pavement and street corner offer another dab of colour to a fascinating picture... His description of his mother's Alzheimer's disease and eventual death are blessed with clarity, gentleness and a heart-wrenching sadness. His memories of shared moments with his father are beautifully rendered... Carson's greatest achievement is recycling a complex mix of emotions and ideas on language into a deeply moving read.'

—Michael Foley, *The Sunday Times*

'For such a tiny book, it is crammed with dozens of stories. Dreams are recounted, the plotlines of adventure books paraphrased and analyzed, poems and song lyrics reprinted, folk stories and urban myths retold. This is a small book, and a hauntingly simple one. *call mother a lonely field* is an immensely pleasurable book, and a valuable addition to the canon of Irish autobiography.'

—Conor O'Callaghan, *The Irish Times*

'*call mother a lonely field* evokes a particular time and dramatic place, as it gets to grips with a society falling apart, all the time making a judicious distinction between archaic loyalties and civilized values. It is written with a vivid economy and understated discernment.'

—Patricia Craig, *Times Literary Supplement*

'A unique poetic meditation on an Irish-speaking family which draws fine threads between language and history and the life-saving properties of a wide-ranging selection of narratives, including family lore, folk songs, comic books and the heroics of mythology which underpin the Irish language. Liam Carson pours an astonishingly concentrated draught of wisdom into one slim volume.'

—Martina Evans

'Carson presents the sights, the sounds, the smells, the essential character of the Falls Road of the period... His mother's descent into Alzheimer's is described with a tenderness that is almost unbearable. Every mother should have a son like this—and indeed it is a lucky child who had parents like his. Liam Carson has done them both proud in this affectionate, haunting, highly readable and, at times, poetic memoir.'

—Maurice Hayes, *Irish Independent*

salmonpoetry

Diverse Voices from Ireland and the World

Belfast Twilight

haiku, senryu and micro-poems

by
LIAM CARSON

Published in 2025 by
Salmon Poetry
Cliffs of Moher, County Clare, Ireland
Website: www.salmonpoetry.com
Email: info@salmonpoetry.com

Copyright © Liam Carson, 2025

ISBN 978-1-915022-96-7

All rights reserved. No part of this publication may be reproduced or transmitted in any form or by any means, electronic or mechanical, including photography, recording, or any information storage or retrieval system, without permission in writing from the publisher. The book is sold subject to the condition that it shall not, by way of trade or otherwise, be lent, resold or otherwise circulated without the publisher's prior consent in any form of binding or cover other than that in which it is published and without a similar condition, including this condition, being imposed on the subsequent purchaser.

Cover Photograph: Dianne Heath
Design & Typesetting: Siobhán Hutson Jeanotte

Printed in Ireland by Sprint Print

Salmon Poetry gratefully acknowledges the support of
The Arts Council / An Chomhairle Ealaíon

in loving memory
of
Ciaran Carson
1948 - 2019

Contents

Introduction   9

Road To The North   13
Belfast Twilight   15
Belfast   16
Belfast Night   22
Spider's Web   25
Dylan At Slane, 1984   27
Mother In Winter   28
Golan Sunset   30
London Graveyard   31
The Buddha's Arms   32
London, 1984   33
Faithful Departed   35
After Jack B Yeats   36
Night Walk   38
Capel Street, Dublin   39
Vanishing Point   40
Mountain's Edge   41
Good Friday 2023, Dún Laoghaire Pier   42
Holy Well, Dalkey   43
Good Friday 2025, People's Park, Dún Laoghaire   44

Séideann An Ghaoth	46
Summer Rain	47
City At Dusk	50
Foggy Day, Dublin	51
Island Haiku (Inis Mór)	52
Island Haiku (Árainn Mhór)	54
Paterson	55
Rainy Day, Dundee	56
Tay Bridge Bar, Dundee	57
Cork Haiku	58
Road To The South	59
Acknowledgments	63
About the Author	64

INTRODUCTION

Sparking Flintstones in the Dark
by Gabriel Rosenstock

Bashō's *Road to the Deep North*, a bible for many haijin, was a deep spiritual calling. An inner journey as much as an outward one. Haiku poetry is nothing but froth without this calling.

In Liam Carson's journey, we follow him to a troubled North, the city that nurtured and reared him – and undoubtedly scared him. The striking and deeply felt haiku in this volume must surely have worked for him as trauma-healing and will, hopefully, do the same for others who were caught up in the Troubles, even peripherally.

Belfast Twilight is a significant contribution to Irish haiku (in both languages – he includes a handful of haiku in the senior language, Irish) and will take its place in world haiku, as well. How could it not? It has mapped out a territory which haiku hasn't entered before, the Northern Ireland Troubles. And it has done so vividly. We are there, in the midst of tumult, in the heart of darkness. After which he brings us South, to where many Northern poets were domiciled.

Haiku has dealt with political scars before. Anti-imperialist haijin were rounded up and persecuted in Japan during the Second World War and some of the most memorable European haiku emerged from the battle-torn Balkans, in such collections as *Knots, The Anthology of Southeastern European Haiku Poetry*, edited by Dimitar Anakiev and Jim Kacian.

Liam Carson's haiku have Heaneyesque echoes here and there:

> ruined cottage
> below its rusted roof
> door into the dark

In a haiku touchingly remembering his late, lamented brother, Ciaran, he glances off Heaney's haiku about his father's walking stick:

> autumn
> wearing my brother's shoes
> i carry his coffin

This has all the hallmarks of great haiku, haiku that is felt, first of all, for if a haiku does nothing more than simply reflect the surface of things, it cannot penetrate the reader; this haiku is lodged in the deep mood of autumn; it speaks in plain, unpoetic language of universal moments that cannot fail to touch us all; and, lastly, it follows Bashō's advice to bring the haiku to our lips, that is to say, it must sound natural, with the music only of the spoken voice to carry it.

> after the graveyard
> a boy sparks flintstones
> in the dark

Liam Carson's haiku, it could be said, 'spark flintstones in the dark'. Powerful, heart-wrenching and inspiring.

Belfast Twilight

Road To The North

the train
hurtling north
swirl of ravens

the train
hurtling north
blood on the tracks

the train
hurtling north
dark skies of Ulster

ruined cottage
below its rusted roof
door into the dark

road to the north
a line of bare trees
on a hillside

road to the north
circus trucks abandoned
in a farmyard

road to the north
the weight of ivy
on a ruined cottage

road to the north
a mansion gazing
on a flooded field

road to the north
a sign pointing
to Blackskull

Belfast Twilight

Belfast twilight
a sound of breaking glass
by the gentle river

Belfast twilight
clouds of starlings pulse
over the Lagan

Belfast twilight
sounds of kick-the-tin
from the street

Belfast twilight
a bonfire's ashes
in the vacant lot

Belfast twilight
the ice cream van's song
from a hidden street

Belfast twilight
the rattle of Lambeg drums
from distant hills

Belfast

alcove under the stairs
toy gun from childhood
dark memory

after the graveyard
a boy sparks flintstones
in the dark

bog meadows
burning bullrushes held high
light the way

bed time story
my father's cigarette
glowing in the dark

smouldering ruins
of Smithfield Market
a young boy weeps

going to school
a soldier's rifle
aimed at my back

three in the morning
helicopter searchlights
comb the city

showers of glass
men with sledgehammers
smash bus windows

back from the seaside
stench of burnt tyres
on the Falls Road

news stand in the rain
beneath a plastic sheet
bright Marvel comics

baseball bats
sold out in the sports shop
punishment beatings

after the bomb
a cloud of bank slips
blows down the road

summer night
my father at the barricade
broomstick in his hand

my mother
recalls the blitz
night sky brighter than day

under the eye
of the security camera
pints in Maddens Bar

helicopter hovers
over a gunman's funeral
endless rain

knock on the door
at three in the morning
shots in the street

the taxi enters
streets I do not know
fear

in the pub
a gunman who could charm
the knickers off a nun

in Clonard monastery
men sing in unison
night falls on Belfast

after the riot
children go hunting
for rubber bullets

not much left
after the bomb
coffin full of bricks

a child sees
body parts shovelled into bags
tea time news

dead of night
my father sorts the mail
in Tomb Street

we play rounders
on Ballycastle beach
Belfast burning

Belfast in spring
a crate of petrol bombs
in a neighbour's garden

republican march
i know i will never be
one of the masked men

into the pub
come the men with guns
Belfast night out

from my bed
i hear my father weep
another murder

bomb goes off
a cloud of glass
hangs in the air

stepping from nowhere
into my mind
the Shankill Butchers

bus stop
psycho with a knife
my brother humours him

a window
bent into a bubble
bang of a distant bomb

metal shutters on the door
wondering why i am
in this strange house

sound of gunfire
from the graveyard
madman on the loose

Belfast mural
light from Christ's hands
falls on the blanket man

hunger strike...
black flags black flags black flags
black everywhere

Belfast in winter
storm winds racing along
the swollen Lagan

Belfast in winter
flowers for a gunman
outside the butcher's shop

mountainside
around a school
snow swirls
on the teacher's fingers
nicotine stains

Belfast Night

Belfast night
wrapped in barbed wire
a man bleeds

Belfast night
fear of a monster
passing car

Belfast night
from a car's boot
a man's moan

Belfast night
shots ring out
dogs bark

Belfast night
at the cave's dark mouth
redcoat's ghost

Belfast night
boy's fear of a bogeyman
under the bed

Belfast night
boy sees himself
as an avenging angel

Belfast night
dragons breath in the sky
helicopters drone

Belfast night
in a window's darkness
face of the Virgin Mary

Belfast night
from an upstairs room
thud of a body

Belfast night
in a man's coat pocket
weight of a gun

Belfast night
by the Lagan's darkness
where monsters dwell

Belfast night
in the gunman's house
shutters slam down

Belfast night
in a garden's darkness
a soldier lurks

Belfast night
behind the fort's steel wall
soldiers gently sleep

shot rings out
in the Belfast night
Johnny was a good man

buses on fire
in the Belfast night
long hot summer

Belfast night
boy dreams of sand yachts
on vermilion sands

Belfast night
the Da strikes a match
a story begins

Spider's Web

night in Dublin
spider's web glitters
in golden street light

little orange bags
of pollen
on the bee's knees

summer night
moth's shadow flickers
inside a lantern

autumn wind
white butterfly
in a swirl of leaves

carried downstream
on the gentle river
sleeping swan

silhouette
of a magnolia tree
bat at dusk

flying in and out
of a ruined warehouse
swifts

so pink
baby rats suckling
on their dead mother

old cottage the stench of a dead sheep

winter sunset an old man's shadow lengthens

sea rippling muscles on a swimmer's back

cuckoo
in the back yard
broken eggs

night falls
a fox's tail slips
into a dark lane

Dylan At Slane, 1984

sun blazes at Slane
Dylan's long black coat
blows in the wind

belting out blues
mascara runs down
Dylan's face

a blazing day
Dylan sings
of no heat in winter

new to Dublin
waft of patchouli oil
in the Dandelion market

Mother In Winter

mother in winter
praying by her mother's photo
a candle flickers

deep winter
threading needles for my mother
the fire glows

winter night
making tea for mother
the kettle's whistle

the coldest winter
mother knits ganseys
for toy soldiers

crisp bank notes
in mother's wrinkled hand
Christmas Eve

winter night
click of knitting needles
my mother prays

swifts in a blue sky
mother scurrying out the door
so long ago

Sunday afternoon rain
mother walks
on and on and on

winter winds
waiting for mother's return
night falls

nursing home
mother pleads to go home
deep winter

winter night
around my dying mother
candles flicker

four coffins
carried out of the nursing home
winter winds

winter winds
on the mountainside
parents' grave

old wardrobe
after all these years
the smell of mother

Golan Sunset

wind blows
through a ghost town
Golan Heights

in the well
a lost sheep drowns
stars come out

on a dusty hill
a burnt out tank
Golan Heights

deep
in the dry valley
a waterfall

Golan Heights
in the blazing sun
a silent minaret

blood flows
from a lamb's slit throat
Golan sunset

bomb shelter
at night
whine of a mosquito

London Graveyard

trembling
on an unmarked grave
a white feather

outliving
all the dead
graveyard oak tree

graveyard walk
the crunch of leaves
underfoot

a wood
at the graveyard's heart
cool shade

green flash
in the evening sky
a parakeet calls

night train
a mother nurses her baby
drizzling rain

The Buddha's Arms

child's grave
a toy rabbit resting
in the Buddha's arms

so bright the geisha
on the streets of Kyoto
roiling rain clouds

deep in the woods
rain keeps falling
a temple

London, 1984

night falls
slow snow in Brixton
forty years ago

snow swirling
outside the Railway Tavern
first night in London

on the tube
sinking into the city
butterflies in the belly

London building site
so many false names
to remember

wee small hours
train crawls through England
stuck in Crewe again

two old queens
mourn Liberace
dust in sunlight

a fug of beer and weed
in the blazing sun
The Pogues in the park

bubble-gum
scent of amyl nitrate
Goth club in Soho

Christmas in the George Canning
Molly the barman
dressed as a fairy

the dealer's hand
green dust
from the sinsemilla

they decide
not to squat the house
evil presence

she flings her boyfriend's drums
out the window
dawn in Peckham

The Pogues at sunset
Shane MacGowan sings
night on fire

Faithful Departed

autumn
wearing my brother's shoes
i carry his coffin

winter walk
along the peaty river
to my nephew's grave

my face reflected
in the bus window
my father

a murmuration of snow
in the street light
souls of the departed

yellow tulips
at the dead man's door
his name unknown

After Jack B Yeats

two men meet
on a dark road
lights of a faraway town

fair day
the bright red lips
of a woman in the crowd

stares into the window
of an empty house
sailor home from the sea

in the heart of the crowd
a woman hears
a tram bell ring

Liffey ferry
looking back at rain
falling on the city

Holyhead at dawn
the ship's passengers
wake from dreams

night train
a woman falls asleep
on her lover's shoulder

in a pub's darkness
a woman sings
of a swallow's wings

on and on
an old man walks
into the silent land

Night Walk

night walk
suddenly a ring
from an empty phone booth

prostitutes' cards
in a phone booth
stench of urine

flaming lighter
in a dark phone booth
someone chases the dragon

abandoned phone booth
wind whistling
through broken windows

Capel Street, Dublin

sunset on Capel Street
voices crackling
from a guard's radio

twilight on Capel Street
in the pink blue sky
cries of seagulls

night on Capel Street
a smoker cups her hands
around a flame

Vanishing Point

mist on the mountain
crows rise
from a bright green field

driving into mist
on this summer's day
flowers at a roadside shrine

four crows look west
bright blaze
of a wheatfield sunset

motorway sunset
car lights enter
the vanishing point

Mountain's Edge

mountain's edge
boarded up windows
house of secrets

mossy walls
of a ruined cottage
deep woods

appears and vanishes
again and again
hillside stream

rusted fence
at the edge of the woods
a black stagnant pool

Good Friday 2023
Dún Laoghaire Pier

Good Friday
still cranes
in the distant city

empty ferry terminal
forgotten emigrants
Good Friday

by the old sea baths
a woman leans on a cross
Good Friday

by the sea
a man struggles up steps
Good Friday

Good Friday
storm clouds gathering
over the seaside town

Good Friday
a man with no saviour
alone on the pier

Holy Well, Dalkey

the sky greys
bright coloured ribbons
on a holy well

man at the well
filling wine bottles
with holy water

man living wild
speaks of holy water
that heals

in the woods
broken bottles and cans
burnt out fires

cliff path
in and out of the brambles
a robin redbreast

Good Friday 2025
People's Park, Dún Laoghaire

wet blackness
of an oak's branches
Good Friday

barely a sinner
in the pouring rain
Good Friday

black tea
and the silent radio
Good Friday

cherry blossom
soaked into a pathway
Good Friday

laughter
from a shuttered café
vinegar on Christ's lips

the cross
of its black wings
crow in rain

the silence
of leaves underwater
Christ's head falls

Christ's last breath
in the pouring rain
starlings rise

Séideann An Ghaoth

madadh leis féin
i gcroílár na hinse
séideann an ghaoth

pléascadh
ón tseanbhalla liath
scornlus corcra

camóg ar an uisce
dobharchú i bhfolach
i ndorchadas na habhann

londubh buí
i measc na gcrann
séideann an ghaoth

fear marbh
a fhidil ina tost
séideann an ghaoth

Summer Rain

summer rain
passing from tree to tree
blackbirds' song

out of its shell
a snail probes
the summer rain

tram stop
wet sleeping bag
draped over railings

tram stop
a man smells of tobacco
and summer rain

summer rain
pile of letters on the floor
empty shop

summer rain
soil getting darker
and darker

summer rain
still missing mother
after twenty years

summer rain
empty deck chair
behind the empty house

wet weight
of drooping leaves
summer rain

summer rain
closed record shop
filling with dust

summer rain
the sound of scaffolding
being dismantled

summer rain
a drunk woman
combs her lover's hair

summer rain
the clunk of the tram
as it switches tracks

summer rain
a line of pigeons follows
a homeless man

blinds drawn
in the funeral home
summer rain

two crows
fight on a rooftop
summer rain

dark day
so bright the lilies
in summer rain

City At Dusk

city's edge
in the travellers' camp
a fire at dusk

city by the sea
a flash of reflected sunlight
from across the bay

shut level crossing
red lights flashing
at dusk

city at dusk
a grey-haired woman
with her greying dog

city at dusk
on the road's edge
abandoned suitcases

city at dusk
a woman photographs
the dying sun

Foggy Day, Dublin

white gull
the laughter of children
vanishes into cold fog

bus running late
in the cold fog
real time stands still

Monkstown
in a bank of fog
ghost of a church tower

street names
in the old Irish script
Blackrock in fog

abandoned coat
on the roadside railing
car tail lights in fog

rugby match
in a shroud of fog
shadows of boys

Dublin after fog
in the bright sunlight
a couple's long shadow

Island Haiku (Inis Mór)

setting sun
in the horse's brown eye
so soft his nose

sunset on the lake
drone of a bee
going home

lowing
of cows at sunset
so still the lake

a fly walks down
the horse's face
twilight

hooks for teacups
on the empty dresser
deserted lighthouse

spiral staircase
rusting in darkness
old lighthouse

Lucky Star Bar
in a cracked window
plastic flowers fade

on the path
to a holy well
a white butterfly

so bright
by the grey stone wall
Alpine strawberry

black back
of a broken currach
island field

Island Haiku (Árainn Mhór)

sheets of rain
a robin shelters
inside a thorny bush

newspaper cuttings
of a long ago drowning
island hotel

old hotel
broken cigarette machine
from bygone days

Paterson

bus driver loves
Emily Dickinson poems
water falls from bright air

where poems are
words written on water
Paterson New Jersey

Aha!
seeing water fall
a poet starts to write

Rainy Day, Dundee

Dundee in the rain
a long dark laneway
to the bright sea

Dundee after rain
women in pink stagger
under a red sky

Dundee after rain
playing cards on the street
another lost game

Dundee after rain
the wee kids' bandstand
all empty now

street corner
homeless girl in a blanket
Dundee after rain

Dundee after rain
under a dripping tree
a drunk girl shouts

Dundee after rain
on a girl's face
a lipstick kiss

Tay Bridge Bar, Dundee

Tay Bridge Bar
glow of yellow light
on whiskey bottles

Tay Bridge Bar
bands of froth
on the emptying glass

Tay Bridge Bar
The Jam on the jukebox
light up a man's memories

Tay Bridge Bar
an electric chandelier
winks on and off

Tay Bridge Bar
a clock ticks away
to the end of the night

Cork Haiku

Sacred Heart ablaze
in a dark shop window
Cork in the rain

sleeping bags hang
from an empty shop's door
Cork in the rain

the Virgin prays
in a roadside grotto
mist on the mountain

scent of oil
the cool darkness
of a country garage

flies on a dead mouse
prayer flags
in a sea breeze

dandelions nod
in a sea breeze
the voice of Buddha

Road To The South
(Wexford train haiku)

sailing one by one
into the eternal sea
swans

from the marshland
into the woods
empty path

Wicklow
the station's Irish name*
hidden by weeds

summer flowers
so bright in a graveyard
a swirl of ravens

just where
the woods get dark
travellers' caravans

blue sky
the black cross
of a grey church

* Cill Mhantáin: Church of the Holy Toothless One.

a foal
kneels by its mother
flow river flow

edge of woods
a woman by a river
her feet in the water

Wexford hills
ghosts of people
burnt in barns

ancient fort
by the broad river
forgotten wars

little boats rust
by the broad river
wind in the rushes

betwixt and between
where river becomes sea
Wexford

raven
circling over me
i am not yours yet

Acknowledgments

I first embarked on the way of haiku with my partner Niamh Lawlor whilst on holiday in Edinburgh, where I bought *Atoms of Delight: an anthology of Scottish haiku and short poems*, edited by Alec Finlay. It is a little jewel of a book. Shortly after, the two of us took to texting haiku to each other.

More than anyone else, I would like to express my heartfelt gratitude to poet and friend Gabriel Rosenstock, the *doyen* of the Irish haiku, both in Irish and English. Many of the haiku in this book were altered on the foot of judicious comments from Gabriel. Thanks are also due to poet Maeve O'Sullivan, whose haiku workshops were invaluable in cutting to the core of what a good haiku is.

I would like to thank editors Gilles Fabre of *seashores: an international journal to share the spirit of haiku* and Caroline Skanne of *hedgerow: a journal of small poems* for regularly publishing my work.

The Irish-language haiku in this book first appeared in the magazine *Comhar*, and thanks are due to its literary editor, Tristan Rosenstock. Buíochas ó chroí.

The title sequence of this book, 'Belfast Twilight', appeared in *Poetry Ireland Review*, and thanks are due to the late Gerald Dawe. Gerry is much missed. Thanks also to Gerry Smyth, poetry editor of the *Irish Times*, for publishing the 'Dylan at Slane, 1984' sequence.

There is no end to the list of people I could thank for their encouragement and valuable feedback. But it would be remiss of me not to mention John Barlow of Snapshot Press, Tess Gallagher, Margaret Lonergan, Paula Meehan, and Jane O'Hanlon. A special thanks goes out to all the members of the Dublin Haiku Salon.

I would like to thank Dianne Heath for kind permission to use her gorgeous photograph on the cover of this book. And a heartfelt thanks to Jim Berkeley for taking publicity photographs.

A special thanks to the lovely staff of The People's Park Café in Dún Laoghaire, where many of these haiku were written. And, of course, thanks to Jessie Lendennie of Salmon Poetry for publishing *Belfast Twilight*; and to Siobhán Hutson Jeanotte for her work on design and typesetting.

Finally, I must thank my partner Niamh Lawlor and our daughter Eithne Carson for their ongoing love and support.

LIAM CARSON is the founder and director of the IMRAM Irish-Language Literature Festival, which stages multimedia literary productions that fuse poetry, prose, visual art and music to promote writing in Irish. He is the author of the critically acclaimed memoir *call mother a lonely field*, shortlisted for the RSL Ondaatje Prize in 2013. He is a haiku poet, and his work has appeared in a wide range of publications, including *Autumn Moon Journal, Comhar, First Frost, hedgerow: a journal of small poems, The Irish Times, Poetry Ireland Review, Presence, seashores, Tiny Words,* and *Wales Haiku Journal*. *Belfast Twilight* is his first haiku collection.

Photograph: Jim Berkeley

salmonpoetry
Cliffs of Moher, County Clare, Ireland

"Publishing the finest Irish and international literature."
Michael D. Higgins, President of Ireland